Dear Hamza Fletc[...]

Enjoy Signing & Keep Sin!
✈ Habiba Yasmin

He yorkshire lad, keep up the awesomeness!
A humble token of appreciation from us brother & sister!
May Allah continually enhance your creativity
and skills so you can be a great source of good for Ummah

May Allah bless you & your family!
Amirul

(Excuse my poor writing... This does not effect
the sincerity of this message. Peace out!)

Published by Amin & Yasmin Ltd 2017

Authors: Aminul Hoque & Habiba Khanam
Illustrator: Rahima Begum © Shroomantics

ISBN 978-0-9957725-0-2

-

*Special thanks to the Deaf Muslim community globally and those striving to support them
with access in their everyday lives and to our family who have seen through our journey.*

*We would also like to thank the BSL interpreting community, our illustrator and all
those involved with this unique project, for their contribution towards the development
and translation of Islamic vocabulary into British Sign Language.*

*We extend our sincere gratitude finally to all the generous donors and
supporters who helped facilitate this unique educational resource.*

May Allah accept from us all Aameen.

Printed by Mega Printing in Turkey

THIS BOOK BELONGS TO

Book

Belong

Practice how to spell your name using
the British Sign Language alphabet below

ALLAH

الله

Raise right index finder
and point towards sky

ANGEL

ملك

One palm on top of other
with thumbs connecting.
Fingers spread outwards
indicating wings.
Slight flapping
of fingertips

BISMILLAH
(In the name of Allah)

بسم الله

Index finger starting at lip.
Raise to right pointing
to sky.

CREATOR

الخالق

Sign letter B.
Then twist and alternate
hands whilst moving
upwards.

DU'A

(Supplication)

دعاء

Hands joined together.
Palms raised upwards
like making Dua.

DATES

تمر

Point index finger to lip.
Rotate downwards.

EID

Start with clenched fist and thumb pointing into left side of chest. Then touch the right side of chest with thumb and hand in the same position

FAMILY

عائلة

Sign letter F.
Then circular rotation
with one hand and
palm downwards.

FORGIVE

Circular motion with closed fist rubbing on open palm of opposite hand.

GUIDE
هدى

One hand to cover and
hold fingertips of other
hand and pull outwards.

HALAL

حلال

Clenched fist with
index fingers pointing
towards each other.
Flick index fingers
downwards twice.

HADITH

حديث

Sign letter H.
Then quotation marks in air.

ISLAM

إسلام

Join middle finger and
thumb, whilst keeping
other fingers open.
Then move hand outwards
and release middle finger.

INSHAALLAH

إن شاء الله

Index finger pointing to sky. Bring down diagonally to open palm.

JUMMAH

جمعة

Thumbs connected.
Fingers outstretched.
Palms facing outwards.
Bring down all fingers
in unison.

JANNAH

جنة

Hands facing each other
above right shoulder.
Branch out both hands.

KA'BAH

كعبة

Hands in front with palms
facing each other.
Turn both palms towards
chest, to indicate box shape.

KNOWLEDGE

علم

Tap thumb to side of forehead with fingers clenched.

LAILATUL QADR
(Night of Power)

ليلة القدر

Hands facing upwards.
Bring hands inwards till
they meet. Then clench fists
and raise arms outwards
indicating strength/power.

MOSQUE

مسجد

Sign letter C like a crescent
moon and place on top
of a closed fist.

MUSLIM

مسلم

Hands joined
together in front.
Palms facing upward
(like making DUA).

NI'MAH
(Blessing)

نعمة

Palms facing downwards
outstretched.
Bring upwards whilst
closing fingertips.

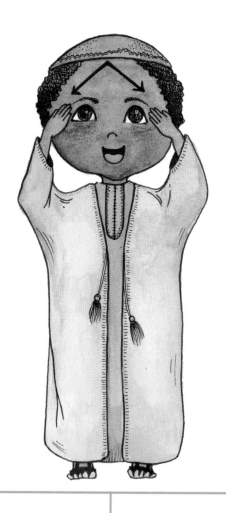

OBEY

أطاع

Fingertips start
center of forehead.
Bring down and outwards.

PATIENCE

صبر

Both palms center of
chest. Stroke downwards
simultaneously

PROPHET

نبي

Sign letter P.
Then both hands raised up
with fingers stretched.
Forward and back motion.

QURAN

قرآن

Sign letter Q.
Then palms together
and open outwards
indicating book.

READ

اقرأ

V shape with index and middle finger. Point to opposite palm and then zigzag motion downwards.

RAMADAN

رمضان

Fingertips on left
side of mouth.
Bring over to right.

SHAHADAH
(Testify)

شهادة

Both index fingers
start at mouth.
Flick outwards with
dip motion.

SUNNAH
(Way of the Prophet)

Withdraw one hand from index finger of other hand whilst closing fingertips.

TAQWA
(Belief and Trust in Allah)

تقوى

Hand upright in front
of face. Bring downwards
to meet open palm.

UMRAH

عمرة

Sign letter U.
One hand closed in front
facing up. Opposite hand
closed facing down. Both
hands circulate.

UMMAH

أمة

Palms facing outwards.
Fingers outstretched.
Rotate outwards
in a circle.

VEIL

Closed hand near chin.
Circulate around head.

حجاب

WUDHU
(Ablution)

وضوء

Bring palm downwards
of clenched fist. Repeat
but opposite hands.

X - ALLAH
KNOWS

الله أعلم

Raise right index finder
and point towards sky.
Tap thumb to side of
forehead with fingers
clenched.

YAWMUL QIYAAMAH

(Day of Judgement)

يوم القيامة

Hands start together and open upwards away from each other. Then clench both fists and alternate up and down twice (like a balance).

ZAM ZAM

زمزم

Sign letter Z. Then break away and meet again to form another Z.

ZAKAT

زكاة

C on top of palm.
Slide C outwards on palm.

Allahu-Akbar
الله أكبر

Raise right index finger and point towards sky. Bring fingers closed together near mouth. Break outwards opening out hands.

SubhanAllah
سبحان الله

Sign letter S. Then right hand above left hand with hands open. Move upwards towards sky with slight shake of hands.

JazakAllah
جزاك الله

Raise right index finger and point towards sky. Fists closed starting from behind shoulder. Bring both forwards over shoulder.

MashaAllah

ما شاء الله

Raise right index finger and point towards sky. Hands facing outwards with middle finger and thumbs touching. Release.

Alhamdulillah

الحمد لله

Thumbs up and move hands in forward circular motion. Raise right index finger and point towards sky.